URSULA BANKS

The Mysterious World of Body Language

The Secret Language We All Speak but Never Learn

Contents

1

Introduction

Body language can be described as the nonverbal communication expressed through physical behaviors, movements, and gestures. It includes facial expressions, posture, hand movements, eye contact, and body positioning. Body language often reveals underlying emotions, attitudes, and intentions, providing cues that complement or contradict spoken words.

Why is this important? Understanding and interpreting body language can help in gaining insights into a person's thoughts, feelings, and attitudes, as well as enhance communication and interpersonal interactions.

My name is Ursula Banks, and in this book, I want to help you understand the power of body language, from interpreting basic cues and what they mean, to decoding the silent signals we all share.

2

The Basics of Body Language

There are several types of nonverbal cues that contribute to body language:

Facial Expressions: The face is a powerful tool for conveying emotions. Facial expressions include smiles, frowns, raised eyebrows, narrowed eyes, and various combinations that communicate happiness, sadness, anger, surprise, disgust, fear, and more.

Gestures: Hand movements and gestures can convey meaning and emphasize spoken words. Examples include waving, pointing, thumbs up, thumbs down, nodding, shaking the head, and various cultural gestures.

Posture and Body Alignment: How a person holds their body and positions themselves can communicate confidence, dominance, submissiveness, openness, or defensiveness. Examples include standing tall with an upright posture, slouching, crossing arms, or leaning forward.

Eye Contact and Gaze: Eye contact plays a crucial role in communication. It can indicate interest, attention, trust, or deceit. Gaze direction, such as looking away or avoiding eye contact, can reveal discomfort, shyness, or dishonesty.

Proximity and Personal Space: The distance we maintain between ourselves and others conveys social and emotional cues. Personal space varies across cultures, but invading someone's personal space or standing too far away can affect comfort levels and communication dynamics.

Touch: Touch can convey a wide range of messages, including affection, support, aggression, or discomfort. Different cultures have varying norms and interpretations regarding appropriate touch.

Voice Tone and Inflection: The way we speak, including tone, volume, pitch, and speed, conveys emotions, attitudes, and intentions. For example, a soft tone may indicate intimacy, while a loud tone may convey anger.

Physical Appearance: Our clothing, grooming, and overall physical appearance can communicate various messages, such as professionalism, social status, personality traits, and cultural affiliation.

It's important to note that the interpretation of nonverbal cues can vary across cultures and individuals, so it's essential to consider cultural context and individual differences when analyzing body language.

3

Understanding Emotional Cues

According to psychologist Paul Ekman, there are six universal emotions that are expressed and recognized across different cultures. These emotions are believed to be innate and evolutionarily adaptive. The six universal emotions are:

1. Happiness: Happiness is expressed through a smile, which involves the upward movement of the corners of the mouth, sometimes accompanied by crinkling at the corners of the eyes.
2. Sadness: Sadness is characterized by a downward turn of the corners of the mouth, often accompanied by drooping or tense facial muscles, lowered eyebrows, and sometimes tears.
3. Anger: Anger is expressed through tightened facial muscles, particularly around the eyes and mouth. The eyebrows may be lowered and drawn together, the lips pressed firmly, and the jaw clenched.
4. Fear: Fear is characterized by widened eyes, raised eyebrows, and an open mouth. The facial expression is often accompanied by a freeze or a defensive posture.
5. Surprise: Surprise involves widened eyes, raised eyebrows, and

an open mouth, but unlike fear, it is typically accompanied by an upward movement of the eyebrows.

6. Disgust: Disgust is expressed through a wrinkling of the nose, an upper lip raise, and sometimes a narrowing of the eyes. It is often associated with an avoidance or withdrawal response.

While these six emotions are considered universal, the intensity and display of these emotions may vary across cultures and individuals. It's also important to note that emotions are complex, and individuals can experience and express a wide range of emotions beyond these six basic categories.

In addition to the six, universal emotions we just discussed, there is also a vast array of micro expressions that we need to be aware of.

A micro expression is a brief, involuntary facial expression that occurs for a fraction of a second. It is a subtle and fleeting display of an emotion that occurs spontaneously before a person can consciously control or mask their true feelings. Micro expressions often occur when an individual experiences a strong emotional reaction, such as surprise, fear, anger, sadness, disgust, or happiness.

Micro expressions are typically very brief and can be challenging to detect, as they occur so quickly. They are considered to be an important nonverbal cue because they reveal genuine emotions that may differ from the emotions a person is trying to portray consciously.

Dr. Paul Beckman, a pioneer in the study of emotions and facial expressions, conducted extensive research on micro expressions. He developed a Facial Action Coding System (FACS), which provides a detailed analysis of facial muscle movements involved in various expressions, including micro expressions. This system has been used to identify and understand the underlying emotions behind micro expressions.

Detecting and interpreting micro expressions can be a valuable skill in fields such as psychology, law enforcement, and negotiations, as they can provide insights into a person's true emotional state or intentions, even when they are trying to conceal or misrepresent their feelings.

4

Interpreting Gestures and Movements

Body language can also encompass a wide range of gestures; nonverbal movements and actions that communicate messages or express emotions. Here are some common body language gestures:

Handshakes: Handshakes are a common gesture used in greetings and professional settings. A firm handshake can convey confidence and trust, while a weak or limp handshake may indicate nervousness or lack of assertiveness.

Nodding: Nodding the head up and down is a gesture used to indicate agreement, understanding, or attentiveness during a conversation. It signals that you are actively listening and engaged in the discussion.

Pointing: Pointing with the index finger can be used to draw attention to something or someone. It can express a directive or indicate a specific object or direction.

Thumbs Up/Down: The thumbs-up gesture is a positive signal indicating approval or agreement, while thumbs down conveys disapproval or disagreement. These gestures are often used to express opinions or to provide feedback.

Waving: Waving is a gesture used to greet or attract attention. It can be a simple hand movement or a more enthusiastic wave of the entire arm, depending on the context and level of familiarity.

Open Palms: Showing open palms is a gesture that signifies openness, honesty, and lack of threat. It can be used to convey trustworthiness or to show that you have nothing to hide.

Crossed Arms: Crossing the arms over the chest is a common gesture that can indicate defensiveness, resistance, or disagreement. It can also be a sign of being closed off or disinterested.

Leaning Forward: Leaning forward during a conversation can signal interest, engagement, and attentiveness. It demonstrates that you are actively involved in the interaction and interested in what the other person is saying.

Shrugging: Shrugging the shoulders is a gesture often used to indicate uncertainty, confusion, or a lack of knowledge or responsibility. It can be accompanied by a facial expression that conveys a sense of "I don't know" or "It's not my problem."

Mirroring: Mirroring is the subconscious imitation of another person's body language and gestures. It can indicate rapport, empathy, and a desire to connect with the other person.

5

Analyzing Posture and Body Positioning

Dominant and submissive postures are body language positions that convey power dynamics and social hierarchy. These postures can indicate the level of confidence, assertiveness, and authority a person holds in a given situation. Here are examples of dominant and submissive postures.

Dominant Postures:

Upright and Open Stance: Standing tall with an upright posture and an open chest suggests confidence and assertiveness. It takes up more physical space and can indicate a sense of authority.

Expanded Body Language: Spreading out limbs, such as placing hands on hips or leaning back with arms stretched out, can project dominance. It displays a willingness to occupy space and be seen.

Head Held High: Holding the head high, with the chin slightly elevated, can indicate self-assurance and dominance. It signifies a sense of pride and control.

<u>Steady Eye Contact:</u> Maintaining direct and steady eye contact can convey confidence and dominance. It demonstrates that a person is unafraid to engage and holds their ground in a conversation or interaction.

Submissive Postures:

<u>Slouched or Hunched Posture:</u> A slouched or hunched posture with rounded shoulders can indicate submissiveness. It makes a person appear smaller and less imposing, potentially conveying deference or timidity.

<u>Crossed or Folded Arms:</u> Crossing or folding the arms across the chest can be a defensive posture but can also signal submission. It can indicate a person's desire to protect themselves or be less confrontational.

<u>Head Tilted Down:</u> Lowering or tilting the head down slightly can indicate submission or humility. It can be a way of showing respect or deference to someone with higher status or authority.

<u>Avoiding Eye Contact:</u> Avoiding or lowering eye contact can be seen as a submissive gesture. It may suggest a person's reluctance to challenge or assert themselves in a given situation.

Nonverbal cues will also frequently indicate interest/attraction. Here are some body language signals associated with **attraction**:

<u>Eye Contact:</u> Maintaining prolonged eye contact can be a strong indicator of attraction. When someone is attracted to another person, they tend to hold eye contact more frequently and for a longer duration. Dilated pupils can also be a sign of attraction.

<u>Smiling</u>: A genuine and frequent smile can be a positive sign of attraction. When someone is attracted to another person, they may smile more often and their smiles may be more pronounced.

<u>Proximity</u>: People who are attracted to each other often try to reduce the physical distance between them. They may lean in closer, find reasons to be near each other, or subtly touch or brush against each other.

<u>Body Orientation</u>: When attracted to someone, individuals may orient their bodies toward the person of interest, facing them directly. This shows openness and engagement in the interaction.

<u>Touch</u>: Light and gentle touches, such as brief hand touches, playful nudges, or brushing against each other's arms, can be indicators of attraction. However, it's essential to respect personal boundaries and gauge the comfort level of the other person.

<u>Playing with Hair or Clothing</u>: Some individuals may exhibit nervous behaviors when attracted to someone, such as playing with their hair, adjusting their clothing, or fidgeting. These actions can be an unconscious attempt to draw attention to oneself.

<u>Open Body Language</u>: Open and relaxed body language, such as uncrossed arms, relaxed posture, and facing the person directly, suggests receptiveness and interest.

<u>Vocal Changes</u>: When attracted to someone, people may experience vocal changes. Their voice may become softer, more soothing, or higher-pitched as they try to create a connection and appeal to the other person.

A person's body language can change based on the specific context and the dynamics of the relationship or interaction. Interpretations of these postures should be made cautiously and in conjunction with other nonverbal and verbal cues to understand the full picture.

6

Contextualizing Body Language

ody Language in Professional Settings

Body language plays a crucial role in professional settings as it can significantly impact how others perceive and respond to you. Here are some key considerations for body language in a professional setting:

Maintaining Good Posture: Sitting or standing with an upright and aligned posture conveys confidence and professionalism. Avoid slouching or slumping, as it can be interpreted as disinterest or lack of engagement.

Strong Handshakes: When greeting colleagues or business associates, offer a firm handshake. A confident and firm handshake can convey professionalism, trustworthiness, and assertiveness.

Making Eye Contact: Maintain appropriate and consistent eye contact during conversations and meetings. It demonstrates attentiveness, interest, and credibility. However, be mindful of cultural norms regarding eye contact, as they can vary.

Using Open Body Language: Keep your body language open and receptive. Avoid crossing your arms, as it can signal defensiveness or disinterest. Instead, keep your arms relaxed and your body facing the person or people you are engaging with.

Active Listening: Engage in active listening by nodding your head, leaning slightly forward, and maintaining eye contact. Show interest and understanding by responding appropriately to the speaker.

Facial Expressions: Be mindful of your facial expressions, as they can influence how others perceive your engagement and emotions. Maintain a pleasant and attentive expression, and be aware of any unintentional negative or distracting expressions.

Gesture Appropriately: Use appropriate hand gestures to emphasize points during presentations or discussions. However, avoid excessive or distracting movements that may detract from your message.

Personal Space: Respect personal space by maintaining an appropriate distance from others. Invading someone's personal space can make them feel uncomfortable or threatened.

Control Nervous Habits: Be aware of any nervous habits, such as tapping your foot, fidgeting, or playing with objects. These behaviors can indicate anxiety or lack of confidence. Practice controlling these habits to project professionalism and composure.

Dress Professionally: Your attire also contributes to your overall professional image. Dress appropriately for the setting and adhere to any dress code requirements.

Remember that body language should align with verbal communication and the specific professional environment. By being mindful of your body language, you can enhance your professional presence, build rapport, and effectively communicate in the workplace.

Body Language in Personal Relationships

Body language plays a crucial role in personal relationships, as it can convey emotions, intentions, and establish connections between individuals. Here are some important considerations for body language in personal relationships:

Physical Touch: Physical touch is a powerful form of nonverbal communication in personal relationships. Appropriate and affectionate touches, such as holding hands, hugging, or gentle caresses, can convey intimacy, warmth, and care.

Eye Contact: Maintaining strong and meaningful eye contact with your partner or loved ones demonstrates attentiveness, interest, and emotional connection. It conveys that you are fully present in the interaction and value the relationship.

Facial Expressions: Expressing genuine and positive facial expressions, such as smiles, softening of the eyes, and raised eyebrows, can convey warmth, love, and happiness. These expressions can foster emotional connection and help convey understanding and empathy.

Body Orientation: When engaging with a loved one, face them directly and align your body towards them. This body orientation indicates openness, attentiveness, and a desire to connect on a deeper level.

Active Listening: Engage in active listening by leaning in, nodding, and responding appropriately. Show genuine interest and empathy through your body language, which helps create a supportive and understanding environment in the relationship.

Mirroring: Mirroring or imitating the body language of your partner can establish a sense of rapport and connection. Subtly matching their posture, gestures, or pacing can create a sense of harmony and unity.

Gestures of Affection: Small gestures like a gentle touch on the arm, a pat on the back, or playing with their hair can express affection and care. These gestures can strengthen the bond and create a sense of closeness.

Respect Personal Space: While physical contact is important in personal relationships, it is equally important to respect personal space and boundaries. Be aware of your partner's comfort level and ensure that your physical proximity respects their boundaries.

Tone of Voice: Pay attention to the tone of your voice when communicating with loved ones. A warm, calm, and soothing tone can create a safe and nurturing environment, while a harsh or dismissive tone can lead to misunderstandings and emotional distance.

Nonverbal Reassurance: Use nonverbal cues to provide reassurance and support, such as gentle pats on the back, a supportive arm around the shoulder, or a tender embrace during times of joy or sadness.

Body language should be aligned with open and honest communication in personal relationships as well. It is essential to be attentive to your partner's nonverbal cues and be receptive to their body language signals, as they can provide valuable insights into their emotions and needs. Building strong and meaningful relationships involves not only verbal but also nonverbal communication through body language.

Body Language in Social Interactions

In addition to professional and personal relationships, body language also plays a significant role in social settings, where the goal is often to establish rapport, build connections, and create a comfortable atmosphere. Here are some important considerations for body language in informal social settings:

Approachability: Maintain an open and relaxed posture to appear approachable. Avoid crossing your arms or creating physical barriers between yourself and others. Instead, keep your arms relaxed and your body language open.

Active Listening: Engage in active listening by maintaining eye contact, nodding, and responding appropriately to what others are saying. Show genuine interest and engagement through your body language to foster meaningful conversations.

Gestures: Use hand gestures to emphasize points or express enthusiasm during conversations. However, be mindful of the cultural norms and context to ensure that your gestures are appropriate and remain respectful.

Personal Space: Respect personal space and maintain an appropriate distance from others. Give people enough room to feel comfortable and avoid invading their personal space, as this can create discomfort or tension.

Leaning In: Leaning slightly forward when engaged in conversation shows interest and engagement. It conveys that you are actively listening and interested in what the other person is saying.

Relaxed Gestures: Use relaxed and natural gestures to express yourself. Avoid excessive or rigid movements that may come across as distracting or overbearing. Keep your gestures fluid and in sync with the conversation.

Tone of Voice: Pay attention to the tone and volume of your voice. Speak clearly, audibly, and at an appropriate volume to ensure that others can hear and understand you. Use a friendly and engaging tone to create a warm and inviting atmosphere.

Remember that body language in informal social settings is about fostering a relaxed and friendly atmosphere. It's important to be genuine, attentive, and respectful in your interactions, allowing your body language to complement your verbal communication. By being aware of your own body language and paying attention to the cues of others, you can navigate social situations with ease and build meaningful connections.

7

Mastering Your Own Body Language

Developing self-awareness is a valuable skill that can enhance personal growth, improve relationships, and contribute to overall well-being. This will be an ongoing practice that requires patience, curiosity, and self-compassion. Here are some strategies to help cultivate self-awareness:

- Embrace Mindfulness: Engage in mindfulness exercises, such as meditation or deep breathing, to cultivate present-moment awareness. Mindfulness allows you to observe your thoughts, emotions, and physical sensations without judgment, helping you gain insight into your inner experiences.

- Practice Emotional Awareness: Pay attention to your emotions and learn to identify and label them accurately. Observe how different situations, people, or thoughts impact your emotional state. Understanding your emotional landscape can provide valuable insights into your inner world.

- Engage in Self-Observation: Throughout your day, make a conscious effort to observe your thoughts, emotions, and behaviors in various situations. Notice any patterns or automatic responses that arise. This practice of self-observation can help you become more aware of your habitual patterns and make conscious choices.

8

Conclusion

Ongoing research holds great potential to further our understanding of human communication and its impact on various aspects of life. As digital communication continues to evolve, there is a growing need to understand how body language translates into virtual interactions. Future research may focus on developing technologies that can accurately capture and convey nonverbal cues in virtual settings, such as video conferences and virtual reality environments.

We can utilize this research to explore cultural variations in body language and develop guidelines to bridge communication gaps, foster understanding, and promote cultural sensitivity.

Because body language can be a reflection of a person's mental and emotional state, we may also be able to explore the connection between body language and mental health conditions, such as anxiety, depression, or trauma. This knowledge can inform therapeutic interventions and enhance mental health assessment and treatment approaches.

From a relationship perspective, understanding body language can help strengthen connections and improve communication dynamics. Future research may delve into how specific body language cues influence relationship satisfaction, conflict resolution, and nonverbal expressions of love and empathy.

Nonverbal behaviors also impact perceptions of leadership effectiveness, authority, and influence in various professional and social settings.

Overall, we have the potential to unlock deeper insights into human communication, improve our understanding of social dynamics, and enhance our ability to connect and communicate effectively in a variety of contexts.

Developing your body language skills can enhance your emotional intelligence, which is the ability to recognize, understand, and manage your own emotions and the emotions of others. By reading and interpreting nonverbal cues accurately, you will gain insights into others' feelings, needs, and intentions. This heightened emotional awareness can help you navigate social dynamics more effectively. Start by becoming more aware of your own body language and gradually incorporate techniques that align with your communication goals. With time and dedication, you will find that applying body language skills can transform your interactions, relationships, and overall presence.

If you found this information helpful, I'd be very appreciative if you left a favorable review for this book on Amazon!

9

Resources

ocial Skills to Read Body Language - Watson Institute. (2023, June 28). Watson Institute. https://www.thewatsoninstitute.org/resource/reading-body-language/

Magazine, V. G.-. B. (2022, October 13). How to Improve Body Language: 20 Tips to Use at Work, at Parties, and When Giving Presentations - Blinkist Magazine. *Blinkist*. Retrieved July 10, 2023, from https://www.blinkist.com/magazine/posts/how-to-improve-body-language

Toastmasters International -Gestures and Body Language. (n.d.). IP. https://www.toastmasters.org/resources/public-speaking-tips/gestures-and-body-language

Six Universal Expressions. (n.d.). https://people.ece.cornell.edu/land/OldStudentProjects/cs490-95to96/HJKIM/emotions.html